MW01142009

SandCastle™

Baby Mammals

It's a Baby Lynx!

Kelly Doudna

Consulting Editor, Diane Craig, M.A./Reading Specialist

ABDO
Publishing Company

Published by ABDO Publishing Company, 8000 West 78th Street, Edina, Minnesota 55439.

Copyright © 2008 by Abdo Consulting Group, Inc. International copyrights reserved in all countries.

No part of this book may be reproduced in any form without written permission from the publisher. SandCastle™ is a trademark and logo of ABDO Publishing Company.

Printed in the United States.

Editor: Pam Price
Content Developer: Nancy Tuminelly
Cover and Interior Design and Production: Mighty Media
Photo Credits: AbleStock, Digital Vision, Eyewire, Peter Arnold Inc. (Manfred Danegger, Steven Kazlowski, J.L. Klein & M.L. Hubert, Bruce Lichtenberger, O. Machill, C. Wermter), ShutterStock

Library of Congress Cataloging-in-Publication Data

Doudna, Kelly, 1963-
  It's a baby lynx! / Kelly Doudna.
      p. cm. -- (Baby mammals)
  ISBN 978-1-60453-025-4
  1. Lynx--Infancy--Juvenile literature. I. Title.

QL737.C23D68 2008
599.75'3139--dc22
                        2007033744

SandCastle™ Level: Fluent

SandCastle™ books are created by a team of professional educators, reading specialists, and content developers around five essential components—phonemic awareness, phonics, vocabulary, text comprehension, and fluency—to assist young readers as they develop reading skills and strategies and increase their general knowledge. All books are written, reviewed, and leveled for guided reading, early reading intervention, and Accelerated Reader® programs for use in shared, guided, and independent reading and writing activities to support a balanced approach to literacy instruction. The SandCastle™ series has four levels that correspond to early literacy development. The levels are provided to help teachers and parents select appropriate books for young readers.

Emerging Readers   **Beginning Readers**   **Transitional Readers**   **Fluent Readers**
(no flags)   (1 flag)   (2 flags)   (3 flags)

SandCastle™ would like to hear from you. Please send us your comments and suggestions.
sandcastle@abdopublishing.com

Vital Statistics

for the Lynx

BABY NAME
kitten, cub

NUMBER IN LITTER
1 to 5, average 2

WEIGHT AT BIRTH
½ pound

AGE OF INDEPENDENCE
10 months

ADULT WEIGHT
22 to 44 pounds

LIFE EXPECTANCY
10 to 17 years

Lynx kittens are born in spring. They are raised by their mothers.

Lynx kittens look like their domestic cousins, house cats.

The mother lynx hides
her kittens under a brush
pile or an uprooted tree.
Rocky crevices also make
good homes.

Lynx communicate with each other the same way house cats do. They meow, purr, and yowl.

Lynx kittens learn to hunt when they are a few months old. A kitten may practice on its mother!

Lynx don't usually chase their prey. They lie in wait and then pounce.

The lynx's main food source is the snowshoe hare.

Lynx are carnivores. Carnivores are meat eaters.

When there are fewer snowshoe hares to hunt, fewer lynx are able to survive.

Lynx have large, furry paws. Their toes spread apart when they walk. This keeps them from sinking into the snow.

Kittens leave their mothers when they are about 10 months old.

Siblings may stay together for a while after they leave their mother. They help each other hunt. That makes it easier for them to survive.

Fun Fact

About the Lynx

A lynx can cover 21 feet in one leap. A snowshoe hare needs four hops to go the same distance!

Glossary

carnivore – one who eats meat.

communicate – to share ideas, information, or feelings.

crevice – a narrow space between two surfaces.

domestic – living with or near humans.

expectancy – an expected or likely amount.

independence – the state of no longer needing others to care for or support you.

pounce – to jump suddenly on something in order to catch it.

prey – an animal that is hunted or caught for food.

sibling – one's brother or sister.

To see a complete list of SandCastle™ books and other nonfiction titles from ABDO Publishing Company, visit **www.abdopublishing.com**.
8000 West 78th Street, Edina, MN 55439
800-800-1312 • 952-831-1632 fax